praying the passion

DAILY READINGS AND PRAYERS FOR LENT
KEN TAYLOR

Kevin
Mayhew

First published in 1996 by
KEVIN MAYHEW LTD
Rattlesden
Bury St Edmunds
Suffolk IP30 0SZ

0 1 2 3 4 5 6 7 8 9

ISBN 0 86209 902 1
Catalogue No 1500077

Cover illustration: *The Last Supper* from
Miroir de l'Humaine Salvation. Bridgeman Art Library,
London, courtesy of Musée Condé, Chantilly.

Design and Artwork by Veronica Ward
and Graham Johnstone
Edited by Peter Dainty
Typesetting by Louise Hill
Printed and bound in Great Britain.

CONTENTS

ABOUT THE AUTHOR

Ken Taylor is a Methodist Minister. Born in Hull and trained in Manchester, he has worked in Orrell, St Helens, Liverpool (Crosby), Leeds (Cross Gates), and Chester-le-Street. He is married, with four sons and a daughter. Recently retired through ill-health, he now lives in Skipton, where he conducts worship and preaches most Sundays.

Died 2010

ACKNOWLEDGEMENTS

The text from the Gospels is from the Revised English Bible and is reprinted here by kind permission of the Cambridge University Press.

The publishers would like to thank Mrs P. E. Dale for permission to reproduce the passages from *New World* by Alan Dale on pages 63 and 83.

INTRODUCTION

A COMPOSITE GOSPEL

None of the four Gospels records all of the 'Seven Words from the Cross' which are at the heart of much Holy Week worship. Mark has only one (which Matthew copied); Luke three; and John another three.

Perhaps the writers did not know of the others; perhaps they did and deliberately chose not to use them.

None of them intended to write a comprehensive account. Gospels were never meant to be biographies or life-stories of Jesus. Gospels are 'preaching' and were written to lead their readers to faith.

Each Gospel is written from the writer's own theological viewpoint. Each painted a word-picture of the Jesus they loved and followed, and they selected, from all that they knew of him, those sayings and stories which best suited their portrait – and omitted the rest.

I find each of these four pictures moving and inspiring and enriching my faith. But for my devotions – and to pray my way through the Passion – I want the fullest and most comprehensive account that I can.

To make such a 'comprehensive narrative' involves doing what the gospel-writers did not do. It means not being selective at all but trying to use every detail and aspect in all four of their pictures. (It also means that *for this purpose only* I have to put their individual theologies and pictures on one side.)

Sometimes, when there are two or more varying versions of the same incident, I have had to be quite arbitrary in which I have used. Sometimes the choice is clear; in others it has been simply by personal preference. Where necessary I have added explanatory notes in Appendix 1.

Using Mark's Gospel as a base (which Matthew certainly did and perhaps also Luke) and interweaving those details which are unique to each of the other three produces the following 'Composite Passion'.

SCRIPTURAL STATIONS

Just as the traditional 'Stations of the Cross' require stopping on the journey for recollection, wonder, and prayer, so I have found, in following this journey from Simon's house in Bethany to the Garden Tomb, very many 'stations' where I have wanted to stop and gaze in wonder or shame.

I have 'paused' in this narrative at those places that speak to me, held that picture in my mind and responded with a prayer. I hope you will find these 'stations' helpful places for you to do the same.

USING THIS BOOK

There are different ways of using this book:

1. There are 46 days in Lent – the traditional 40 'fast' days and the six Sundays (which are festival days and not officially for fasting).

I have arranged this composite gospel so that there is a reading and a prayer for each day from Ash Wednesday to Easter – if you prefer to use it that way.

2. This journey, step by step in the way of the Cross, has proved helpful in public worship as well as private devotion. A programme of how this has been used on the evenings of Holy Week is set out in Appendix 3 on page 111.

3. It will also prove helpful at some point to read the whole narrative of the Passion – using just the left-hand pages – straight through at a single sitting.

And there are other ways. Whichever you choose, I hope it will help to bring you nearer to the heart and mind of Christ.

K.T.

Praying the Passion

It was before the Passover festival, and Jesus knew that his hour had come and that he must leave this world and go to the Father. He had always loved his own who were in the world, and he loved them to the end.

John 13:1

Daily prayer

Father,
as in heart and mind
we follow step by step
the path that Jesus trod,

help us to see more clearly
the full extent of his love

and to find in you
forgiveness and healing,
refreshing and renewal,
strengthening and peace,

through the love
which you make plain in Jesus.

Ash Wednesday
PLOTTING

It was two days before the festival of Passover and Unleavened Bread, and the chief priests and the scribes were trying to devise some scheme to seize him and put him to death.

'It must not be during the festival', they said, 'or we should have rioting among the people.'

Mark 14:1-2

Also Matthew 26:3-5; Luke 22:1-2; John 11:47-53.

We heartily condemn them, Lord,
– but we understand them very well.

We've been exposed to the same temptations.

They weren't the first – or the last –
    to want to preserve their own status and authority.

And we understand their arguments very well:
    we've heard them so often in councils and committees.

We feel uncomfortable
    when we examine their methods;

    we too are afraid of anything
    that seems to threaten us.

And there are people
    we would prefer to exclude from our associations.

And, not to put too fine a point on it,
    we sometimes devise schemes
    to use other people

    or try to manipulate those close to us.

In this season of penitence,
    as we see something of ourselves in them,
    have mercy upon us;

    forbid that we should ever use our powers
    for our own ends;

    nor let us ever, ever, exclude *anyone*,
    – for that would mean excluding you.

Day 2

ANOINTING

Jesus was at Bethany, in the house of Simon the leper.

As he sat at table, a woman came in carrying a bottle of very costly perfume, pure oil of nard. She broke it open and poured the oil over his head.

Some of those present said indignantly to one another, 'Why this waste? The perfume might have been sold for more than three hundred denarii and the money given to the poor'; and they began to scold her.

But Jesus said, 'Leave her alone. Why make trouble for her? It is a fine thing she has done for me. You have the poor among you always, and you can help them whenever you like; but you will not always have me. She has done what lay in her power; she has anointed my body in anticipation of my burial. Truly I tell you: wherever the gospel is proclaimed throughout the world, what she has done will be told as her memorial.'

Mark 14:3-9

Also Matthew 26:6-13; John 12:1-8 names Judas and Mary.

Lord,
    why is it that we get jealous so easily
    of someone else's perception
    or sensitivity
    or generosity?

It's not only among your first disciples:
    it happens among us still,
    often,
    far too often.

We have to admit:
    we ourselves are among the 'poor',
    for there are so many ways
    in which we are impoverished.

We all need you to recall us
    to what really matters.

Mary is an inspiration to us:

    we want to be more like her,

    to take your words to heart,

    to be more sensitive to what you are doing

    and to pour out for you
    the very best that we have.

Day 3

JUDAS

Then Judas Iscariot, one of the Twelve, went to the chief priests to betray him to them.

When they heard what he had come for, they were glad and promised him money;

and he began to look for an opportunity to betray him.

Mark 14:10-11

Also Matthew 26:14-15; Luke 22:3-6; John 13:2.
See note 1 (page 102)

It wasn't the money, was it, Lord?

Did he want to force your hand?

He'd heard you talk so much about the kingdom
 and longed for it to come as much as you:

  – though his idea of the kingdom
  was so very different from yours.

Was he trying to make it happen?

Did he think that putting you on the spot
 would make you have to act decisively,
 dramatically?

Perhaps he'd prayed about it;

  certainly he had thought long about it;

  and he was so sure that he was right!

Have mercy on us, Lord,
 when we do the same.

From where we stand,
 and as far as we can see,
 we generally think *we* are right.

And when we pray
 we often try to make you do what we want,
 urge you to do what we want done,
 implore you to give us what we're sure we need.

Lord, teach us to pray;
 teach us what 'in your name' means.

Day 4

SECRET SIGNS

Now on the first day of Unleavened Bread, when the Passover lambs were being slaughtered, his disciples said to him, 'Where would you like us to go to prepare the Passover for you?'

So he sent off two of his disciples with these instructions: 'Go into the city, and a man will meet you carrying a jar of water. Follow him . . .

'. . . and when he enters a house give this message to the householder: "The Teacher says, 'Where is the room in which I am to eat the Passover with my disciples?'"

'He will show you a large upstairs room, set out in readiness. Make the preparations for us there.'

Then the disciples went off, and when they came into the city they found everything just as he had told them. So they prepared the Passover.

Mark 14:12-16

Also Matthew 26:17-19; Luke 22:7-13; John: Eve of Passover. See note 2 (page 102).

That was all very secret, Lord!

Real 'cloak-and-dagger' stuff:
    secret signs and signals,
    and a secret house,
    and nobody knowing where.

Was it all simply to make sure
    that you were not disturbed by the police?

So that no one could betray you
    till you were ready?

Is what you wanted to say and do
    with your friends
    so very important
    that it must not be interrupted?

When we come to your table,

    help us to take to heart what you say

    and treasure all your secret meanings,

Make what you say and do
    at your table
    most important for me,
    in the secret places of my heart.

JERUSALEM AT LAST

When the hour came he took his place at table, and the apostles with him;

and he said to them, 'How I have longed to eat this Passover with you before my death!

'For I tell you, never again shall I eat it until the time when it finds its fulfilment in the kingdom of God.'

Luke 22:14-16

This saying is recorded only by Luke.
See note 3 (page 103)
For how the following scriptures best fit into the traditional Passover Seder see page 108.

Jerusalem, at last, Lord!

After all your long and patient waiting,
   the time has come,
   the time you chose.

You decided
   it must be at Passover –
   and Passover has come!

Soon you can set in motion
   the machinery of law and order:
   it is all moving inexorably
   to the end that you must dread.

The long patience
   and waiting in the wilderness
   are over . . .
            . . . Jerusalem at last!

Be patient with me, Lord!

I'm not very good at patience,

   or at waiting . . .

   . . . especially upon you,

   and I find it very hard
   deliberately to choose
   the way of love.

Teach me the deep meanings of your Passover

   and may your kingdom be fulfilled in me!

Day 6

A JEALOUS DISPUTE

Then a dispute began as to which of them should be considered the greatest.

But he said,
'Among the Gentiles, kings lord it over their subjects; and those in authority are given the title Benefactor. Not so with you: on the contrary, the greatest among you must bear himself like the youngest, the one who rules like one who serves.

'For who is greater – the one who sits at table or the servant who waits on him? Surely the one who sits at table. Yet I am among you like a servant.

'You have stood firmly by me in my times of trial; and now I entrust to you the kingdom which my Father entrusted to me;

'in my kingdom you shall eat and drink at my table and sit on thrones as judges of the twelve tribes of Israel.'

Luke 22:24-30

This narrative in Luke is parallel to John's account of the feet-washing (see Day 7).

That's a good start, Lord!

I suppose they were all a bit edgy,
   with so much secrecy,
    . . . and all the tension,
    . . . and being in Jerusalem again,
    . . . and no servant at the door even!

But we can't excuse it
   by saying it was the wine speaking,
   – not this early in the evening!

How many times do you have to tell them?

How many times do you have to tell us?

It's going to take more than words!

Your promises
   about sitting at your table
   are very reassuring,

   . . . but somehow
   servanthood and thrones
   don't seem to fit together.

Teach me,
   . . . show me,
   . . . give me
   the humility
   that is the heart of the kingdom.

Day 7

FEET-WASHING

During supper, Jesus, well aware that the Father had entrusted everything to him, and that he had come from God and was going back to God, rose from table, took off his outer garment and, taking a towel, tied it round him.

Then he poured water into a basin, and began to wash his disciples' feet and to wipe them with the towel.

When he came to Simon Peter, Peter said to him, 'You, Lord, washing my feet?'
Jesus replied, 'You do not understand now what I am doing, but one day you will'.
Peter said, 'I will never let you wash my feet'.
'If I do not wash you,' Jesus replied, 'you have no part with me.'
'Then, Lord,' said Simon Peter, 'not my feet only; wash my hands and head as well!'

Jesus said to him, 'Anyone who has bathed needs no further washing; he is clean all over; and you are clean, though not every one of you'. (He added the words 'not every one of you' because he knew who was going to betray him.)

After washing their feet he put on his garment and sat down again.

'Do you understand what I have done for you?' he asked. 'You call me Teacher and Lord, and rightly so, for that is what I am. Then if I, your Lord and Teacher, have washed your feet, you also ought to wash one another's feet. I have set you an example: you are to do as I have done for you.'
John 13:3-15

See note 4 (page 103).

Lord,
    I still find it hard to accept
    the idea of a humble God.

The Father of whom you teach me
    is not the kind of God that I expect at all.

The ways of your kingdom
    are so different from what I expect

    . . . and very different from what *they* expected.

It's hard to see you on your knees –
    not exalted but on your knees –
    on your knees
    at my service,
    at my disposal.

And I'm not surprised at Simon
    trying to make it a kind of sacrament.

It's hard to accept the reality,
and the humility, of the Servant-King.

And it's even harder to humble myself.

I don't mind serving some people
. . . those I love and like
. . . most of the time,

but to serve anyone at all,
including those I don't like,
– that's hard.

I like to be selective in my service.

Help me.

Day 8

PREDICTING BETRAYAL

As they sat at supper Jesus said, 'Truly I tell you: one of you will betray me – one who is eating with me'.

At this they were distressed; and one by one they said to him, 'Surely you do not mean me?'

'It is one of the Twelve', he said, 'who is dipping into the bowl with me. The Son of Man is going the way appointed for him in the scriptures; but alas for that man by whom the Son of Man is betrayed! It would be better for that man if he had never been born.'

(Mark 14:18-21)

The disciples looked at one another in bewilderment: which of them could he mean?

One of them, the disciple he loved, was reclining close beside Jesus. Simon Peter signalled to him to find out which one he meant. That disciple leaned back close to Jesus and asked, 'Lord, who is it?'

Jesus replied, 'It is the one to whom I give this piece of bread when I have dipped it in the dish'. Then he took it, dipped it in the dish, and gave it to Judas son of Simon Iscariot. As soon as Judas had received it Satan entered him. Jesus said to him, 'Do quickly what you have to do'. No one at the table understood what he meant by this. Some supposed that, as Judas was in charge of the common purse, Jesus was telling him to buy what was needed for the festival or to make some gift to the poor.

As soon as Judas had received the bread he went out. It was night.

John 13:22-30

Also Matthew 26:20-25; Luke 22:21-23.
See note 5 (page 104).

Is it I, Lord?

Is it I who betrays,
    who denies,
    who sleeps when you say 'Stay awake',
    who flees when there is danger?

Is it I
    who calls you Lord
    and then doesn't do what you say;
    who builds on sand?

Is it I, Lord?

Lord, have mercy.

There's Judas
    on your left,
    in the specially trusted,
    specially honoured place,
    receiving the privileged sandwich . . .

Doesn't make any difference though,
    does it, Lord?

Deliver me
    from being so determined,
    so sure I'm right,
    so set in my ways,

    that when I'm wrong
    you cannot change my mind.

Help me to open my mind,
    as well as my heart,
    to you.

Day 9

A NEW COMMAND

When he (Judas) had gone out, Jesus said, 'Now the Son of Man is glorified, and in him God is glorified. If God is glorified in him, God will also glorify him in himself; and he will glorify him now.

'My children, I am to be with you for a little longer; then you will look for me, and, as I told the Jews, I tell you now: where I am going you cannot come.

'I give you a new commandment: love one another; as I have loved you, so you are to love one another. If there is this love among you, then everyone will know that you are my disciples.'

John 13:31-35

Only John records this conversation and saying.

It sounds quite simple
   when you say it, Lord,

   but to love one another as you love us
   is not as easy as it sounds.

When we work out what it means
   – always patient, always kind,
   no envy or boasting, no conceit or rudeness,
   no selfishness, no score of wrongs,
   no limit to faith or hope or endurance
   – it's very hard for us.

Being 'commanded' is not enough,
   we need more than that;

   even your clear example is not enough,
   we need more than that;

   we need some *help*.

Can it be
   that this is *promise* as well as command
   at the same time?

When you command, 'You must love one another'
   are you also promising, 'You *will be able to*'?

Is the secret of it, 'You in me' and 'I in you',
   when you are working in our lives?

Lord Jesus, fill me with your love,
   – until there is no room in me
   for anything that spoils me,
   no room for anything save Love.

THIS BREAD OF SACRIFICE

During supper he took bread,
and having said the blessing
he broke it and gave it to them,
with the words:
'Take this: this is my body.'

Mark 14:22

Also Matthew 26:26; Luke 22:19.
See note 6 (page 104).

So this is the reason
   for the secrecy, Lord:

     not only for a new command,
     but for new sign and symbol,
     and new meaning.

The Passover bread of sacrifice
   is now sign of your sacrifice.

Whether they had roast lamb that night or not,
   you yourself are the Lamb,
   the Lamb slain from the foundation of the world.

This now is sign and symbol
   of your self-offering,
   laid wide open,
   exposed,
   vulnerable.

And not only sign and symbol,
   it is sacrament:
   our oath of allegiance to you

   and means of your grace to us.

Lord, as you opened the bread
   and opened yourself to us,

   help me to open myself to you,
   open my hands,
   open my heart.

Day 11

THE NEW COVENANT

Then he took a cup, and having offered thanks to God he gave it to them; and they all drank from it.

And he said to them,
'This is my blood,
the blood of the covenant, shed for many.

'Truly I tell you: never again shall I drink from the fruit of the vine until that day when I drink it new in the kingdom of God.'

Mark 14:23-25

Also Matthew 26:27-29; Luke 22:17-18.

I wonder,
   in that upper room,
   and as tradition bids . . .

   did you pour a cup for Elijah, Lord,
   when he is come already,
   and the way prepared already,
   and the kingdom at hand?

You give your own new meaning
   to the last cup, too:

   the traditional cup of covenant
   is now sign and symbol and sacrament
   of your new Covenant.

Long looked for
   and always needed,
   the ancient hope becomes reality:
   and we hold in our hands
   what Jeremiah dreamed of.

Now by your dying and self-giving love
   is your new law written on our hearts
   and within them.

Lord,
   as we pour out our wonder and our love to you,
   pour your love in our hearts;

   write your new law of love upon our hearts;

   and as you come to live in us,
   so may we live in you.

See note 7 (page 104)

Second Sunday

TABLE TALK

'Simon, Simon, take heed: Satan has been given leave to sift all of you like wheat; but I have prayed for you, Simon, that your faith may not fail; and when you are restored, give strength to your brothers.'

He said to them, 'When I sent you out barefoot without purse or pack, were you ever short of anything?' 'No', they answered. 'It is different now,' he said; 'whoever has a purse had better take it with him, and his pack too; and if he has no sword, let him sell his cloak to buy one. For scripture says, "And he was reckoned among transgressors", and this, I tell you, must be fulfilled in me; indeed, all that is written of me is reaching its fulfilment.' 'Lord,' they said, 'we have two swords here.' 'Enough!' he replied.

Luke 22:31-32; 35-38

After singing the Passover hymn, they went out to the Mount of Olives.

Mark 14:26

In the long Seder of Passover there would be much more 'Table talk'. John 14 to 17 (which is not printed here) relates to that, but needs special study, considering John's style and method.

This precious meal with many conversations
   is coming to an end;

   the ominous darkness closes round
   and you begin to warn them . . .

   but they didn't understand, did they, Lord?

Still talking about swords,
   after all this time with *you*
   – and your teaching of non-violence!

Simply mention the word 'sword'
   and the old ingrained ideas
   come quickly to the surface.

Such shallow grasp of what you teach
   is more than disappointing.

But I don't really understand either,
   . . . perhaps I don't want to.

Indoctrinated prejudice and childhood hates
   are slow to yield to you.

Let your love reach to the heart of me
   – and *change* me, Lord.

Like Simon I am sifted;
   sometimes my faith is shredded!

          Pray for ME, Lord

I want to help my brothers,
   but I need your love to strengthen me.

Day 13

PREDICTING DENIAL

After singing the Passover hymn, they went out to the mount of Olives.

And Jesus said to them, 'You will all lose faith; for it is written: "I will strike the shepherd and the sheep will be scattered". Nevertheless, after I am raised I shall go ahead of you into Galilee.'

Peter answered, 'Everyone else may lose faith, but I will not.'

Jesus said to him, 'Truly I tell you: today, this very night, before the cock crows twice, you yourself will disown me three times'.

But Peter insisted: 'Even if I have to die with you, I will never disown you'.

And they all said the same.

Mark 14:26-31

Also Matthew 26:30-35; Luke 22:33-34 and John 13:36-38.

I do what Simon did, Lord:

I make great promises to you;
   then find it hard to keep them.
Forgive me.

'Even if everyone else . . .', he said.
I do that too . . . we all do . . .

We compare ourselves to other people
  – dare to judge their achievements and failures
  – and privately think we're better than they are.
Have mercy on us.

Help me to accept myself realistically:

   help me to accept my limitations,
   and stop me longing for what is beyond me;

   and help me to accept my real potential.

Show me
   how loving and gentle, patient, caring, and faithful
   I could be if I would – *can* be with your help.

Lord, help me become what I am meant to be.

Great and good Shepherd,
   struck down for my sake,
   do not let me fall from faith . . .

   even in the most frightening times,
   do not let me fall from faith.

Day 14

REACHING GETHSEMANE

When they reached a place called Gethsemane, he said to his disciples, 'Sit here while I pray'.

And he took Peter and James and John with him.

Horror and anguish overwhelmed him, and he said to them, 'My heart is ready to break with grief; stop here and stay awake'.

Then he went on a little farther, threw himself on the ground, and prayed that if it were possible this hour might pass him by.

'Abba, Father,' he said, 'all things are possible to you; take this cup from me. Yet not my will but yours.'

Mark 14:32-35

Also Matthew 26:36-39; Luke 22:39-42.

You just wanted their company
   didn't you, Lord?

Not only for their sakes
   but for *your* sake . . .

   in the darkness and the wrestling.

There are times for all of us
   when we simply need
   the company of our friends.

Thank you for the people
   who 'company' us:

   for those closest to us,
   for those who share with us,

   especially when we're in trouble.

As we remember them now,
   and name them
   in the stillness of our hearts,

   and bless you for them,

   bless each of them
   according to their need.

Day 15

IN THE GARDEN

He came back and found them asleep;

and he said to Peter,
'Asleep, Simon? Could you not stay awake for one hour?

'Stay awake, all of you;
and pray that you may be spared the test.
The spirit is willing but the flesh is weak.'

Once more he went away and prayed.

On his return he found them asleep again,
for their eyes were heavy;
and they did not know how to answer him.

Mark 14:37-40

Also Matthew 26:40-43

Waken your church, Lord!

We cry to you to rouse yourself
— 'Arm of the Lord, awake!'

We urge you to do something
about the mess we've got ourselves into . . .

and all the time
it is we who are asleep!

We don't take your warnings to heart;
we don't really take your promises to heart;
we say 'Lord, lord' and don't do what you say.

Have mercy on us;

Waken us to love;

Help us to see what you have *already* done
about the mess that we are in

and help us to recognise
what you are doing now,
in the world today,

and stir ourselves to work with you.

Waken us to love!

Day 16

AGONY

He went away a second time and prayed:

'My Father,
if it is not possible for this cup to pass me by
without my drinking it,
your will be done.'

Matthew 26:42

And now there appeared to him an angel from heaven bringing him strength, and in anguish of spirit he prayed the more urgently;

and his sweat was like drops of blood falling to the ground.

Luke 22:43-44

He came again and found them asleep, for their eyes were heavy.

So he left them and went away again and prayed a third time, using the same words as before.

Matthew 26:43-44

Lord,
   we're wide awake now,
   but we can't share this;

   all we can do is watch,
   holding our breath with wonder.

You go into a deeper darkness
   than we can imagine,

   searching for the Father
   in the deep, deep darkness,

   trying to find a meaning
   in all you know is waiting,

   and wanting to be able
   to accept what you find.

We sense you on the edge
   of a black abyss –

   wrestling with desolation,
   assailed by doubt,
   ravaged by despair,
   facing death . . .

   and we know that the battle is joined.

Our darknesses are pale
   alongside this deep darkness of yours,
   but we know many kinds of darkness
   and they can be very frightening.

Jesus of Gethsemane,
Good Shepherd risking all for us,
   when we are in the dark
   hold us secure.

Day 17

ARREST

He came a third time
and said to them,
'Still asleep? Still resting?
Enough! The hour has come.
The Son of Man is betrayed into the hands of sinners.
Up, let us go! The traitor is upon us.'

He was still speaking when Judas, one of the Twelve, appeared,
and with him a crowd armed with swords and cudgels, sent
by the chief priests, scribes, and elders.

Now the traitor had agreed with them on a signal: 'The one
I kiss is your man; seize him and get him safely away.'

When he reached the spot, he went straight up to him and
said, 'Rabbi', and kissed him.

Then they seized him and held him fast.

Mark 14:41-46

Also in Matthew 26:45-50 and Luke 22:47-48.
On John's account see note 8 (page 104).

You ought to know, Lord,
    that's typical of police raids:
    secrecy, speed, surprise, and sudden assault . . .

    and the place surrounded so no one can escape
    when the prey are wakened,
    drowsy, puzzled, and off-guard.

And there was Judas, so excited,
    his schemes fulfilled:
        'Now, Lord, you have no choice:
        you are surrounded.
        Now, Lord, you have to act.
        Call for the angels!
        Bring in the kingdom!
        Now, Lord!',
    striding to greet you with a kiss.

But you, my Lord, are in control, not they:
    handing yourself over,
    laying down your life . . .

'Let these men go'
    was not what they expected,
    not Judas, nor the soldiers, nor your friends.

Lord, you laid down your life
    that we might go free.

Deliver me from the dangers I am in;

    set me free to be what I am meant to be;
    set me free to love;

    and, as you gave yourself for me,
    help me give myself to you.

Day 18

HEALING

When his followers saw what was coming they said, 'Lord, shall we use our swords?'

And one of them struck at the high priest's servant, cutting off his right ear.

But Jesus answered, 'Stop! No more of that!'

Then he touched the man's ear

and healed him.

Luke 22:49-51

Also in Matthew 26:51-54; Mark 14:47; John 18:10-11; but only Luke records the healing.

Lord, this is marvellous . . . really.

He comes to hurt you . . . and you *heal* him.

'Love your enemies', you said
　　. . . and you did!

Quite wonderfully,
　　in the dreaded darkness
　　of this time and place,
　　there is this light of healing love.

Wherever *you* are
　　there is always healing, light, and love.

Thank you for the healing you bring
　　even to me;

　　not hurt for all my hurting you,
　　but healing.

Thank you for all
　　through whom you give healing to us.

We pray for all who need healing now,
　　all who are hurting today,
　　all whom we are naming in our hearts:

　　touch them too with your healing love.

Third Sunday
DESERTION

Then Jesus spoke,

'Do you take me for a robber, that you have come out with swords and cudgels to arrest me?

Day after day I have been among you teaching in the temple, and you did not lay hands on me.

But let the scriptures be fulfilled.'

Then the disciples all deserted him and ran away.

Among those who had followed Jesus was a young man with nothing on but a linen cloth.
They tried to seize him; but he slipped out of the linen cloth and ran away naked.

Mark 14:48-52

Also in Matthew 26:55-56; Luke 22:52-53; John 18:4-9.

That's Mark, Lord, that was!

It's good to know he was there,
    teenage eyewitness,
    following from his mother's house
    in the secrecy of the bushes;
    it underlines his later record,
    a signature to his gospel.

I can understand his running away.

They all ran away:
I can understand that very well too.

But what is almost beyond my understanding
    is you, Lord:

I saw you wrestling with doubt
    and all those other dark forces;

    now you stand
    calm, controlled, caring, confident,

    handing yourself over
    to the agents of those same dark forces.

Now you are utterly alone
    . . . and go deeper into the darkness
    . . . beyond where we could go
    . . . for our sakes.

Such love is too wonderful for me.

Jesus of Gethsemane, I adore you.

Day 20

TO ANNAS

The troops with their commander, and the temple police, now arrested Jesus and secured him.

They took him first to Annas, father-in-law of Caiaphas, the high-priest for that year – the same Caiaphas who had advised the Jews that it would be to their interest if one man died for the people.

Jesus was followed by Simon Peter and another disciple. This disciple, who was known to the high priest, went with Jesus into the courtyard, but Peter stayed outside at the door. So the other disciple, the high priest's acquaintance, went back and spoke to the girl on duty at the door, and brought Peter in.

John 18:12-16

Also in Matthew 26:57-58; Mark 14:53-54; Luke 22:54.

No comment, Lord.

In our hierarchies,
    the higher echelons of church authority,
    whom you know can matter more than what;
    and it is not unknown among us,
    like Annas, to keep it in the family!

Nor is it unknown among us
    for those in authority or government
    to compromise a principle
    in their own interest,
    or to sacrifice someone else
    for what suits them . . .
                . . . and call it expedient.

We pray for all in authority over us:

    foster integrity in them,
    deliver them from self-interest,
    confound corruption,
    and sustain them when the decisions are hard.

And again we pray for our families,
    those whom we know best
    who matter most to us.

We are so concerned about their wellbeing
    that perhaps we are too earthbound
    and shortsighted in our hopes for them.

As we name them one by one
    and hold them in our faith and love,

    we pray
    the best that can possibly be for them.

Day 21

INTERROGATION

The high priest questioned Jesus about his disciples and his teaching.

Jesus replied,
'I have spoken openly for all the world to hear;
I have always taught in synagogues or in the temple, where all Jews congregate;
I have said nothing in secret.
Why are you questioning me? Question those who heard me; they know what I said.'

When he heard this, one of the police standing near him struck him on the face. 'Is that the way to answer the high priest?' he demanded.

Jesus replied, 'If I was wrong to speak what I did, produce evidence to prove it; if I was right, why strike me?'

So Annas sent him bound to Caiaphas.

John 18:19-24

Only John records this interrogation.

Your proper protest makes the point, Lord.

They know very well what you taught;
   they have detailed reports;

   but they're frightened of you, Lord,

     afraid you might cause division,
     and they want to preserve unity;

     afraid you will challenge their authority,
     and respectability,
     and status in the community.

And most of all
   they are afraid you will undermine
   their traditions and their institution;
   and they don't want change.

We are like them.

We know what you teach,
   but are afraid to take it to heart.

We keep you at arm's length
   in case you disturb our peace.

You call us to be agents of transformation
   but we don't really want to be disturbed.

Have pity on us:
   help us to trust you enough
   to let your love work in us
   and transform us.

Day 22

TRIAL

As soon as it was day, the elders of the people, chief priests, and scribes assembled, and he was brought before their Council.

Luke 22:66

The chief priests and the whole Council tried to find some evidence against Jesus that would warrant a death sentence, but failed to find any.

Many gave false evidence against him, but their statements did not tally.
Some stood up and gave false evidence against him to this effect: 'We heard him say, "I will pull down this temple, made with human hands, and in three days I will build another, not made with hands".'
But even on this point their evidence did not agree.

Then the high priest rose to his feet and questioned Jesus: 'Have you no answer to the accusations that these witnesses bring against you?' But he remained silent and made no reply.

Mark 14:55-61

Also in Matthew 26:59-63.

This silence is very impressive, Lord.

Harshly dealt with, he bore it humbly;
  he never opened his mouth.

You just stand there,
  like a sheep that is dumb before its shearers
  . . . it's very impressive.

It's so natural to want to explain,
  to want to be understood,
  to try to justify oneself . . .
  but you don't, Lord . . .
        . . . you don't need to, do you?

This silence is very impressive.

We could learn from your silence.

Sometimes we speak
  when it would be better to stay quiet.
Sometimes we say things
  that would be better left unsaid.
Sometimes we say things we regret afterwards,

  and sometimes we keep quiet
  when it would be better to speak out.

Lord, teach us
  when to be quiet,

  and *how* to be quiet,

  and when we speak, Lord,
  teach us how to speak in love,
  to speak only in love.

Day 23

JUDGEMENT

The high priest then said,
'By the living God I charge you to tell us:
are you the Messiah, the Son of God?'

Jesus replied,
'The words are yours.
But I tell you this: from now on you will see the Son of Man
seated at the right hand of the Almighty and coming on the
clouds of heaven.'

At these words the high priest tore his robes and exclaimed,
'This is blasphemy!
Do we need further witnesses?
You have just heard the blasphemy. What is your verdict?'

'He is guilty,' they answered; 'he should die.'

Then they spat in his face and struck him with their fists;
some said, as they beat him, 'Now, Messiah, if you are a
prophet, tell us who hit you'.

Matthew 26:63-68

Also in Mark 14:61-65 and Luke 22:63-71.
See note 9 (page 105).

That reaction is frightening, Lord!

They're so afraid of you
   it brings out the worst in them.

What's most frightening for us Lord,
   is that they were good people:

     guardians of orthodoxy,
     defenders of the faith,
     with the highest moral and spiritual insights
     of any yet . . .
     and they react like this!

They were devout men,
   moderate men,
   good men . . . some were friends of yours . . .
   and they were unanimous!

You warned us, didn't you, Lord,
   how standing orders can become too rigid,
   how rules and regulations can limit Love,
   can crib, confine, and crucify Love?

Let this be a warning to us!

As we see you, calm and controlled,
   standing for faith and hope,
   for truth and love . . .

   let it bring out the *best* in us!

Day 24

DENIAL

Peter [had] followed at a distance.

They lit a fire in the middle of the courtyard and sat round it, and Peter sat among them.

A serving-maid who saw him sitting in the firelight stared at him and said, 'This man was with him too'. But he denied it: 'I do not know him', he said.

A little later a man noticed him and said, 'You also are one of them'. But Peter said to him, 'No, I am not'.

About an hour passed and someone else spoke more strongly still: 'Of course he was with him. He must have been; he is a Galilean.' But Peter said, 'I do not know what you are talking about.'

At that moment, while he was still speaking, a cock crowed;

and the Lord turned and looked at Peter.

Peter remembered the Lord's words, 'Tonight before the cock crows you will disown me three times'.

And he went outside, and wept bitterly.

Luke 22:54-62

Also in Matthew 26:69-75; Mark 14:66-72; and John 18:25-27.

How he wished he'd kept quiet:
   and you like a sheep before the shearers.

Poor old Simon and his big mouth!
Making promises
   that he couldn't keep
   when the chips were down.

He was so impetuous, wasn't he, Lord?
   ... but he was as loyal to you as anyone,
   followed you further than any other
   – as he promised

But he'd been asleep –
   woke bewildered ... stunned ... frightened ...
   and tried to follow you.

How he wished he'd kept quiet!
The guilt was terrible:
   he would never forgive himself.

He only managed to hold on,
   to regain his balance,
     ... eventually to accept your forgiveness
        ... and at last even to forgive himself,

   because of the look in your eyes, Lord,
   as you caught his eye
   across the courtyard;

   because of the compassion, the understanding,
   the forgiving look in your eye.

Catch my eye, Lord!
   hold me by your compassion
   your understanding and forgiveness
   now!

Day 25

DESPERATION

When morning came . . . they bound him and led him away, to hand him over to Pilate, the Roman governor.

When Judas the traitor saw that Jesus had been condemned, he was seized with remorse, and returned the thirty silver pieces to the chief priests and elders.

'I have sinned,' he said; 'I have brought an innocent man to his death.'

But they said, 'What is that to us? It is your concern.'

So he threw the money down in the temple and left; he went away and hanged himself.

Matthew 27:1-5

Only Matthew records this incident.

I feel sorry for Judas, Lord.

All right, he chose what he was going to do,
   he decided . . . and did it,

     but was he so much worse
     than any of the others, Lord?

'Judas the traitor', they said;
   but they were glad of a scapegoat:
   it made them feel less guilty.

Yes, I know, he betrayed them too.

But *you* could have forgiven him,
   couldn't you, Lord?

You were ready to forgive anyone,
   if only, like Peter,
   they would accept your forgiveness.

By the same mercy that held Peter
   you could have forgiven Judas
   . . . couldn't you, Lord?

No one was more remorseful than he was
   but . . .
     . . . oh, that's the saddest thing, isn't it?
     he didn't understand you well enough,
     didn't know you well enough,
     despaired of your love,
     thought he was beyond forgiveness.

Let me never despair of your love.

Help me to know you well enough
   to know that there is nothing,
   nothing that is beyond your forgiving.

PILATE

From Caiaphas Jesus was led into the governor's headquarters.

It was now early morning, and the Jews themselves stayed outside the headquarters to avoid defilement, so that they could eat the Passover meal.

So Pilate came out to them and asked, 'What charge do you bring against this man?'

They opened the case against him by saying, 'We found this man subverting our nation, opposing the payment of taxes to Caesar, and claiming to be Messiah, a king'.

Pilate asked him, 'Are you the king of the Jews?'

He replied, 'The words are yours'.

Pilate then said to the chief priests and the crowd, 'I find no case for this man to answer'.

But they insisted: 'His teaching is causing unrest among the people all over Judaea. It started from Galilee and now has spread here.'

When Pilate heard this, he asked if the man was a Galilean, and on learning that he belonged to Herod's jurisdiction he remitted the case to him, for Herod was also in Jerusalem at that time.

John 18:28, 29
Luke 23:2-7

Also in Matthew 27:11, 12; Mark 15:1-5.

What is the truth about Pilate, Lord?

Was he capable and competent,
  or weak and unimaginative,
  or ruthless and hard?

Was his appointment to this explosive province
  a down-grading for previous mistakes?

And this was too much for him, wasn't it?

He neither liked nor understood
  your countrymen or their leaders.

They'd bettered him three times already
  and he was wary of them.

Irritated to be dragged out before dawn,
  he then comes face to face with *you*
  – and he knows he's got a problem;

  but when they mention Herod
  he can see a loophole to avoid a difficult decision.

We pray for all in authority over others:

  for all faced with difficult decisions today;

  for all in the grey world of politics,
  where a good compromise
  is the best they can hope and work for;

  for all who have to work
  with people they don't like;

  and in the choices I have to make today
  guide me by your truth and love
  and help me.

Day 27

HEROD

When Herod saw Jesus he was greatly pleased; he had heard about him and had long been wanting to see him in the hope of witnessing some miracle performed by him.

He questioned him at some length without getting any reply;

but the chief priests and scribes appeared and pressed the case against him vigorously.

Then Herod and his troops treated him with contempt and ridicule, and sent him back to Pilate dressed in a gorgeous robe.

Luke 23:8-11

Only Luke records this incident.

What about Herod then, Lord?

A devout Jew, who denied his faith
   by his actions and his immorality.

His reputation is that he's superficial, Lord,
   only interested in being entertained,
   only concerned about current fashions
   and present trends.

And you just stood there.
This silence is not so impressive, it's sad.

When there's nothing you can say
   to get through to a man
   because he's so superficial, it's very sad.

He wanted you to perform a miracle;
   and *I* would like you to perform a miracle!

Not magic,
   no sophisticated conjuring trick,
   but one of *yours*, a real miracle.

I'm astonished and thrilled to see how
   you are breaking down barriers.

So what about the gulf between North and South?
   Will you please create a willingness
   in all of us who have far more than we need
   to share justly with all who have almost nothing?
That will take a real miracle!
               – which only you can handle.

And please, Lord,
   I would like a miracle for *me* –
   will you please make me more trusting,
   . . . and more loving?

Day 28

A RECONCILIATION

That same day Herod and Pilate became friends;

till then there had been a feud between them.

Luke 23:12

This is recorded by Luke only.

Lord, one of your recent disciples said:
    'People who couldn't get on with one another
    found it possible to be friends in his presence.'

And it works!

You really can make peace!

And now we see you breaking down barriers
    which we thought would never fall
    – though we prayed for it to happen!

Earnestly we pray for the breaking down of barriers,
    for the dispelling of fear and suspicions
    and for lasting peace,

    wherever there is long division or discord,
    wherever people are estranged
    or find it hard to get on with one another.

We pray for true reconciliation
    between nations,
    between races,
    between generations,
    between sexes,
    between churches,
    and between religions;

    and whatever these prayers mean
    that we ourselves must be and do,
    give us the grace we need.

From *New World* by Alan Dale (OUP)

See note 10 (page 105).

Day 29

CROWD REACTION

Pilate now summoned the chief priests, councillors, and people, and said to them, 'You brought this man before me on a charge of subversion.
'But, as you see, I have myself examined him in your presence and found nothing in him to support your charges. No more did Herod, for he has referred him back to us. I therefore propose to flog him and let him go.'

But there was a general outcry. 'Away with him! Set Barabbas free.'

Pilate addressed them again, in his desire to release Jesus, but they shouted back, 'Crucify him, crucify him!'

For the third time he spoke to them:
'Why, what wrong has he done? I have not found him guilty of any capital offence. I will therefore flog him and let him go.'

But they persisted with their demand, shouting that Jesus should be crucified.

Luke 23:13-23

John gives special treatment to the Pilate confrontation. See note 11 (page 105).

Chief priests and Sanhedrin councillors, yes;
    but not *all* the people, surely, Lord?
    Not that early in the morning.

Were the others 'rent-a-crowd',
    with rabble-rousers positioned by the priests
    to sway the mood?

Were none of your friends and followers there
    or those who shouted 'Hosanna!'?

Surely not all people are as fickle as that?
Or are we naive about crowd dynamics?

It's easy to feel lost and alone in a crowd;

    it's so easy to be carried along
    and to accept what everyone else is saying;

    and we are manipulated more than we realise
    by advertising and marketing and polls.

Help me keep my wits about me;
    and save me from going with the crowd
    till I know where they're going.

We praise you with all the crowds of heaven.

We pray for all who feel lost or alone in a city,
    and all whose voice is never heard.

We pray for calm in crowds of people
    shopping, in traffic jams,
    at sports meetings and in demonstrations.

And for the crowds of refugees we pray help.

Day 30

BARABBAS

At the festival season it was customary for the governor to release one prisoner chosen by the people.

There was then in custody a man of some notoriety, called Jesus Barabbas.

When the people assembled, Pilate said to them, 'Which would you like me to release to you – Jesus Barabbas, or Jesus called Messiah?'

For he knew it was out of malice that Jesus had been handed over to him.

Meanwhile the chief priests and elders had persuaded the crowd to ask for the release of Barabbas and to have Jesus put to death.

So when the governor asked, 'Which of the two would you like me to release to you?' they said, 'Barabbas'.

'Then what am I to do with Jesus called Messiah?' asked Pilate; and with one voice they answered, 'Crucify him!'

'Why, what harm has he done?' asked Pilate;
but they shouted all the louder, 'Crucify him!'
Matthew 27:15-18, 20-23

Also in Mark 15:6-14; Luke 23:19-25; John 18:39, 40.

Now there's irony, Lord:
    you both have the same name!

Jesus Barabbas, or, Jesus, Son of Abba!

Why did they choose the wrong one?

Barabbas must have laughed himself sick!

No wonder you wept over this city
    that put its trust in armed force.

But why do we always choose the wrong one?

Why do we want a man of action,
    someone who'll get things done quickly?

Why do we settle for violent action?

Why do we *force* people to do what we want?

We pray for all oppressed people,
    for all who suffer violence,
    for terrorists and all who inflict violence.

Give me the courage I need
    to stand for what is just and true
    and to live your way of non-violence.

    and for God's sake
    deliver me from any malice or spite!

Day 31

HAND-WASHING

While Pilate was sitting in court a message came from his wife: 'Have nothing to do with that innocent man; I have been much troubled on his account in my dreams last night.'

When Pilate saw that he was getting nowhere, and that there was danger of a riot, he took water and washed his hands in full view of the crowd.

'My hands are clean of this man's blood', he declared. 'See to that yourselves.'

With one voice the people cried, 'His blood be on us and on our children'.

Matthew 27:19, 24-25

These incidents are recorded by Matthew only.

You stand facing Pilate, Lord,
   and it's clear who's in chains!

You stand calm, controlled and *free*.

And Pilate is starting to panic, isn't he?

He's tried every escape –
   – Herod, belligerent refusal, Barabbas, ridicule –
   but the decision has to be his.

Whatever his wife said doesn't help at all –
   the final decision is his.

He can hear what they are saying
   and the open threats . . .
   and he daren't offend them again.

He's made too many mistakes already;
   and his career is on the line.

He knows that you are innocent
   – but he's too weak or cynical or afraid.

And that hand-washing is pathetic:
   we can't avoid responsibility like that, can we?

Help us accept responsibility
   for the harm we've done.
Forgive us
   and help us try to make amends.

And give us the freedom within ourselves
   to stand for truth and justice,
   even when it's costly.

Day 32

SCOURGING

Pilate, in his desire to satisfy the mob,
released Barabbas to them;

and he had Jesus flogged,

and then handed him over to be crucified.

Mark 15:15

Also in Matthew 27:26; Luke 23:25; John 19:1, 16.
See note 12 (page 105).

That was totally unjust, Lord,
    and quite unnecessary.

Now you suffer
    to satisfy another's guilt and hostility,

      . . . and I can almost feel the soldier
    getting the anger out of his system!

We all victimise other people
    for our own frustrations and disappointments.

We have fears and resentments
    we find it hard to bear . . .
    and take it out of someone else.

Lord, when someone hurts me,
    I want to hit back.

You don't –
How do you take it?
How do you stop it going any further?
How do you stop and stem and transmute and
    transform the hurt?

Now we see what Love does with suffering:
    lets it do no more harm.

Now we can only 'stop, and gaze, and fall, and own . . .
    was never love like thine!'

Fifth Sunday

MOCKING

Then the soldiers of the governor took Jesus into his residence, the Praetorium, where they collected the whole company round him.

They stripped him and dressed him in a scarlet cloak;

and plaiting a crown of thorns they placed it on his head, and a stick in his right hand.

Falling on their knees before him they jeered at him: 'Hail, king of the Jews!'

They spat on him, and used the stick to beat him about the head.

Matthew 27:27-30

Also in Mark 15:16-19; Luke 23:11; John 19:2-3.
See note 13 (page 106).

I suppose they thought it was funny, Lord.

You looked quite ridiculous, you know,
   – a thornbush stuck upside down on your head.

Why do we make fun of people?
Why do we laugh at them behind their backs,
   expose them to ridicule
   when they can't hit back?

Their idea of a king, even a comic one,
   is very different from yours;
   why do we try to make people
   fit our idea of what they ought to be?

And they focus all their anti-Semitism on you.

What is it that brings out the worst in us
   when we're in a gang?

We pray for all people
   who are exposed to ridicule,
   exploited or abused.

And we watch you in awe and wonder:

'Abused, you did not retort with abuse;
   suffering, you uttered no threats' –
   this is breathtaking.

How do you do that?

How do you accept it all
   and leave it for God to use?

Day 34

TO GOLGOTHA

When they had finished their mockery, they stripped off the purple cloak and dressed him in his own clothes.

Then they led him out to crucify him.

Mark 15:20

And he went out, carrying the cross himself, to the place called The Skull (in Hebrew, 'Golgotha').

John 19:17

Also in Matthew 27:31
See note 14 (page 106).

I'm glad that they allowed you
   to be yourself, Lord,
   in the clothes that you chose,
   for the path that you chose.

Not someone else's picture of you,
   or their idea of what a king should look like,
   or their idea of what glory is,
   or their narrow idea of love even.

Now we can see you yourself
   as you really are.

Paul was right:
   we can see the glory of God
   in your face . . .
   tired and worn, bruised and bleeding,
   we can see true glory.

And now
   as your passion unfolds before us
   we can see what is truth:
   the truth about God,
   the truth about ourselves,
   the truth about sin,
   and the truth about Love,
   your forgiving, healing, redeeming Love.

Blessed Lord,
   help us to see and understand.

Day 35

THE WAY OF THE CROSS

As they led him out to crucify him, a man called Simon, from Cyrene, the father of Alexander and Rufus, was passing by on his way in from the country, and they pressed him into service to carry his cross.

Mark 15:21
also Matthew 27:32

Great numbers of people followed, among them many women who mourned and lamented over him.

Jesus turned to them and said, 'Daughters of Jerusalem, do not weep for me; weep for yourselves and your children.

'For the days are surely coming when people will say, "Happy are the barren, the wombs that never bore a child, the breasts that never fed one". Then they will begin to say to the mountains, "Fall on us", and to the hills, "Cover us".

'For if these things are done when the wood is green, what will happen when it is dry?'

Luke 23:27-31 (only)

See note 15 (page 106).

Slowly through the narrow streets,
　　you climb the long, slow hill of your love,

　　weakened by that flogging,
　　staggering with the weight of that heavy beam,
　　and on your strong shoulders
　　all the burden of the world.

Simon, coming into the city, is horrified at the scene
　　and looks with pity at your stumbling, Lord.

He must have been afraid
　　when they grabbed him from the crowd
　　and made him carry your cross.

We know little else about him, Lord.

When you reached the hill, did he stay to watch
　　or slip trembling away as soon as he could?

Did this unexpected path change his life's direction?

Did he see you crucified and hear your prayer;
　　and did he (and his family) come to faith?

We pray for all who carry heavy burdens
　　. . . or share another's;

　　for those who stumble under what they have to bear,
　　or find it hard to keep going . . .
　　and we pray help for them.

Give us the grace to bear one another's burdens;
　　and if *our* life takes an unexpected turn,
　　help us to keep on following you.

Day 36

CRUCIFIXION

Coming to a place called Golgotha (which means 'Place of a Skull'), they offered him a drink of wine mixed with gall; but after tasting it he would not drink.

When the soldiers had crucified Jesus they took his clothes and, leaving aside the tunic, divided them into four parts, one for each soldier.
The tunic was seamless, woven in one piece throughout; so they said to one another, 'We must not tear this; let us toss for it.' Thus the text of scripture came true: 'They shared my garments among them, and casts lots for my clothing.'
That is what the soldiers did.

Two bandits were crucified with him, one on his right and the other on his left.

Matthew 27:33
John 19:23-24
Matthew 27:38

Also Mark 15:23-24.

Redeeming Lord,
    the Cross now dominates our sky.

Such brutality and cruelty are offensive to our eyes,
    but we dare not turn away from this
    as you come to your throne.

Many can hardly believe what they are seeing;

    but the barracking priests are here,
    harrowing you till you are dead;

    and soldiers, too familiar with this distasteful duty,
    are dicing for their 'perks';

    and the women who attend so many crucifixions
    have brought their sour wine;

    but you, my Lord, have none of it
    – you want a clear head to handle what is coming . . .
    and show us how you deal with suffering.

Crucified Lord, you are not high and exalted,
    for this low cross is coarse and crude,
    but you *are* 'lifted up'.

and you are still where we will always find you:
    . . . with the outcasts,
    . . . in the midst of those who are suffering,
    . . . alongside the dying.

At the foot of your Cross
    we pray for all who are outcast,
    all who are suffering today,
    all who are dying now.

And for ourselves at the foot of your Cross we pray.
Help us to hear what you are saying to us.

Day 37

INSCRIPTION

Pilate had an inscription written and fastened to the cross; it read, 'Jesus of Nazareth, King of the Jews'.

This inscription, in Hebrew, Latin, and Greek, was read by many Jews, since the place where Jesus was crucified was not far from the city.

So the Jewish chief priests said to Pilate, 'You should not write "King of the Jews", but rather "He claimed to be king of the Jews"'.

Pilate replied, 'What I have written, I have written'.

John 19:19-22

Also in Matthew 27:37; Mark 15:26; Luke 23:38.
See note 16 (page 107).

Was this a deliberate gibe at the priests,
    a petulant insisting that he had the last word?

Was he still unnerved by meeting you,
    and not sure about your kingdom?

Or, as happens so often with us,
    did he not realise the full force of what he wrote?

In effect, of course,
    what he has written and nailed up still stands,
    I.N.R.I. still proclaims your name and nature.

It's ironic
    that a Roman who does not believe in you
    has testified to your kingship – in three languages!

Now your cross stands against the sky;
    the Father's love is 'earthed',
    a placard till the end of time.

Now you are lifted up
    and can begin to draw all people to yourself,
    – not only Jews and Romans and Greeks,
    but all of us.

Crucified Lord,
    we praise you
    for the sure, strong, steady love
    that has brought you to this place
    and manifests your kingdom.

As we are drawn to you, and call you King,
    rule in our lives.

Day 38

FORGIVENESS

Jesus said: 'Father, forgive them; they do not know what they are doing.'

Luke 23:34

Luke alone records this saying.
See note 17 (page 107).

Crucified Lord,
    they say you *kept on praying,* 'Father forgive them'.

Was it like a mantra, constantly repeated,
    gritting your teeth
    against the pain of hammered nails?

Your first crucified 'word' stresses
    that forgiveness is essential.

And you told us so often:
    that forgiveness must be *unlimited,*
    or else it will turn back into violence.
    ('70 times 7 times', you said.)

Only by forgiveness
    can we live together in peace
    or in harmony with God.

Crucified Lord,
    we *never* know what we're doing!

We don't realise how much hurt we add
    to the web of the world's need and pain:
    have mercy upon us and forgive us.

Cluttered around the foot of the Cross,
    we see sins like our own;
    for we are Caiaphas, Judas, Pilate and the rest:
    have mercy upon us and forgive us.

Forgive my sins, Lord – all my sins.
Here, at the foot of the Cross,
    let your forgiving word
    reach to the very heart of me.

From *New World* by Alan Dale (OUP)

TO PARADISE

The passers-by wagged their heads and jeered at him: 'Bravo!', they cried, 'So you are the man who was to pull down the temple, and rebuild it in three days! Save yourself and come down from the cross.'

The chief priests and scribes joined in, jesting with one another: 'He saved others,' they said, 'but he cannot save himself. Let the Messiah, the king of Israel, come down now from the cross. If we see that, we shall believe.'

Even those who were crucified with him taunted him.

One of the criminals hanging there taunted him: 'Are you not the Messiah? Save yourself, and us.'

But the other rebuked him:
'Have you no fear of God? You are under the same sentence as he is. In our case it is plain justice; we are paying the price for our misdeeds. But this man has done nothing wrong.'

And he said, 'Jesus, remember me when you come to your throne'.

Jesus answered, 'Truly I tell you: today you will be with me in Paradise'.

Mark 15:29-32
Luke 23:39-43

Also in Matthew 27:39-44; Luke 23:35-37.

Forgiving Lord,
    whether he was simply showing sympathy
    or realised who you are,
    whether patronising or penitent,
    he turns to you;

    – and you are there, of course,
    with compassion, understanding, and hope;

    just as you are always there
    whenever we turn to you
    – and always offering hope:
    'Take the next step with me'.

For him it was a step into life eternal;
    but your invitation is not only at the end of the line:
    but whenever, wherever, we turn to you.

We pray for those we know at the end of the line,
    whom you have now brought to the gate of paradise.

We pray for those who are at the end of their tether,
    who can see no hope at all.

I dare not say, 'Lord, remember me'
    for you have never forgotten me,
    although, betimes, I have forgotten you;

    and you are with me always,
    'to the end of time', you said;
    and so, at the end of my time, you will be there.

Not only then but now, today,
    help me take the next step with you;
    and, whatever comes next,
    let me go forward – with you – in hope.

Palm Sunday

HIS MOTHER

Meanwhile near the cross on which Jesus hung, his mother was standing with her sister, Mary wife of Clopas, and Mary of Magdala.

Seeing his mother, with the disciple whom he loved standing beside her, Jesus said to her,
    'Mother, there is your son';

and to the disciple,
    'There is your mother';

and from that moment the disciple took her into his home.
John 19:25-27

This is recorded by John alone.

Lord of love and sorrow

'A sword shall pierce your soul', said Simeon,
   and it does;

   but she stays there,
   remains with the pain
   in fellowship with your sufferings.

We are moved, but not surprised,
   by the streams of love that flow between you;
   your deep concern and care for her
   despite your pain,

   and for your closest friend.

You give them to each other,
   for they need each other;
   need to accept each other's help and love.

No wonder some have seen
   sign and symbol of the church
   in this gracious bonding.

   for you have given *us* to each other
   in the wisdom of your care for us,
   to give and take help amongst us,
   and to love one another.

We pray for your church,
   the fellowship where we belong,
   and all your Christians,

   and we pray for our family and friends,
   those who share our need and pain
   and stand with us.

Day 41

DARKNESS

At midday a darkness fell over the whole land, which lasted till three in the afternoon;

and at three Jesus cried aloud,

      'Eloi, Eloi, lema sabachthani?'

which means, 'My God, my God, why have you forsaken me?'

Mark 15:33-34

This saying is also recorded by Matthew (27:45-46).
The three hours' darkness is also recorded by Luke (23:44-45).
See note 18 (page 107).

Crucified Lord,
 this darkness is frightening
 and you are utterly alone.

You hear the Temple trumpets heralding the Passover,
 but you are outcast and excluded from them both,

  excluded from the holy city,
  outcast from your kinsfolk,

  and in this deep, deep darkness
  it seems that even God has forsaken you
  – left you to suffer all the agony alone;

  utterly alone,
  under the fierce assault of all the powers of evil
  and suffering all the burden of our sin,

  in darkness and doubt, dereliction and despair,
  and dying – alone.

This is way beyond anything we can understand,
 but, with the whole creation, we hold our breath
 while the battle is joined
 and all hangs in the balance.

Lord, does that great despairing cry
 mean that, even in the utter darkness,
 you cling for comfort to familiar psalms,
 while faith hangs on by the skin of its teeth?

Have mercy on us for bringing you to this;
 and hear our prayer
 for all who are outcast or lonely or despairing.

Day 42

THIRST

After this, Jesus, aware that all had now come to its appointed end, said in fulfilment of scripture,

'I am thirsty'.

A jar stood there full of sour wine; so they soaked a sponge with the wine, fixed it on hyssop, and held it up to his lips.

John 19:28-29

Only John records this saying.
Parallel versions about the wine are recorded in Matthew 27:48 and Mark 15:35-36.

Crucified Lord,

   so many hours' suffering
   and this the only glimpse you give us
   of the reality of the physical pain.

And we cannot escape the feeling
   you are moistening your lips
   for what comes next!

St John and many others
   see sign and symbol of so much more:

   of your many associations with water,

   and a sign of all our thirsting,
   all our needs and all our good desires,
   our longing for you – and your longing for us.

Most simply, you are thirsty near the end
   and ask your enemies' compassion;
   and help is given from that unlikely quarter.

We pray for all who are really thirsty,
   for all who thirst for righteousness,
   for all who long for justice and peace.

And because we all need help from others,
   give us the humility we need to accept it
   gratefully,
   – even from the most unexpected people.

And make us ready, like that soldier,
   to respond to any whispered call for help.

Day 43

IT IS ACCOMPLISHED

A jar stood there full of sour wine;

so they soaked a sponge with the wine, fixed it on hyssop, and held it up to his lips.

Having received the wine, he said,

'It is accomplished'.

John 19:29-30

Only John records this saying.

Love is so vulnerable and precarious
that it was always possible that Love would fail;
but you, dear Lord, have not stopped loving . . .

and your great cry of victory
echoes against the darkened sky.

Your work is done.
It is accomplished!

O Saviour of the world,
what you have done for us is wonderful and true.

You have achieved

victory,
and Love is proved supreme;

a perfect sacrifice,
the self-offering of the Suffering Servant;

true revelation,
and the only Son has made plain
the Father's heart of love;

atonement,
for the Temple veil is sundered
and we have clear access to the Father;

reconciliation,
and we may now be reconciled to God;

and a New Covenant,
so that now God can work in our lives.

You have accomplished more than we can understand!

Liberating Lord, this is breathtaking.
We stand in awe and wonder – and adore you.

Day 44

CONFIDENCE

Jesus uttered a loud cry
and [then] said,

   'Father, into your hands I commit my spirit';

   and with these words he died.

Luke 23:46

Only Luke records this saying.

Redeeming Lord,

    are we back with the psalms again?

Is this the childhood prayer
    you learned and said each night –

    as you quietly bow your head,
    and close your eyes,
    and trust everything to the Father,
    as if you were going to sleep?

Loving Lord,
    this above all we have learned from you:

    that God is Abba,
    our Father, and we can trust him;

    and that for us, as for you,
    everything begins and ends with Abba,
    for everything is in his hands
    – and we can trust him.

You came to this hill
    determined more than confident,
    but now all is accomplished.

You have finished your work
    and now commit it all to Abba,
    put everything in his hands
    and trust it to him.

For, as you taught us,
    all things finally are in his hands
    – life, and death, and beyond death,
    all things.

Abba, help *us* to trust you more
and dare to trust all things to you.

GOOD FRIDAY

It seems fitting on this day to read again
all the gospel pages from Day 36

With these words he died.

And the curtain of the temple was torn in two from top to bottom.

When the centurion who was standing opposite him saw how he died, he said, 'This man must have been a son of God'.

The crowd who had assembled for the spectacle, when they saw what had happened, went home beating their breasts.

A number of women were also present, watching from a distance. Among them were Mary of Magdala, Mary the mother of James the younger and of Joses, and Salome, who had all followed him and looked after him when he was in Galilee, and there were many others who had come up to Jerusalem with him.

Luke 23:46
Mark 15:38-39
Luke 23:48
Mark 15:40-41

Also in Matthew 27:51-56 and John 19:31-37; with their own theological significance.

In this way,
    on a day like this,
    on a hill outside the city,
    amid barracking and ridicule,
    humiliation, hatred, and scorn,
          Jesus Christ died;
    accepting suffering to transform it,
    bearing sin to redeem us,
    and deliver us from all the evil
    that prevents us becoming what we are meant to be.

Now stands the Cross

Here at the foot of the Cross
    are cluttered all our sins and fears;

    and here we can lay all our needs and cares,
    all our worries and burdens.

Here we can hear him speaking,
    – and one word is especially for me, today:

    he speaks forgiveness and hope and company,
    sharing and help, victory and peace

        Let what you say to me
        reach to the very heart of me.

        The way is made plain,
        and the times have turned,
        and all is in Love.

BURIAL

When evening fell, a wealthy man from Arimathea, Joseph by name, who had himself become a disciple of Jesus, approached Pilate and asked for the body of Jesus; and Pilate gave orders that he should have it.

Joseph took the body, wrapped it in a clean linen sheet, and laid it in his own unused tomb, which he had cut out of the rock. He then rolled a large stone against the entrance and went away.

Mary of Magdala was there, and the other Mary, sitting opposite the grave.

Next day, the morning after the day of preparation, the chief priests and the Pharisees came in a body to Pilate. 'Your excellency', they said, 'we recall how that impostor said while he was still alive, "I am to be raised again after three days". We request you to give orders for the grave to be made secure until the third day. Otherwise his disciples may come and steal the body, and then tell the people that he has been raised from the dead; and the final deception will be worse than the first.'
'You may have a guard,' said Pilate; 'go and make the grave as secure as you can.'
So they went and made it secure by sealing the stone and setting a guard.

Matthew 27:57-66

See also Mark 15:42-47; Luke 23:50-56; John 19:38-42.

Father,
    look in pity on all your grieving children.

Joseph of Arimathea,
    bitterly regretting his failure
    to stand and speak until it was too late,

    finds courage to admit his own discipleship
    and lay his Lord quietly to rest, now it is all over.

It seems all over. Jesus is dead.
His words seem empty, his promises broken,
    and all their hopes in him are shattered.

In this stunned shock,
    Mary is weeping,
    Peter unconsolable,
    John is very quiet,
    and they and all his friends need time to grieve.

They talk of yesterday,
    and happier days and memories
    of what their Master said and did;

    . . . in a strange limbo till tomorrow
    and their last acts of love for him.

We pray for all who are grieving today.

We pray for all regretting
    what they have not said or done until it is too late.

We pray for all still struggling with bereavement
    of weeks or months or years ago;

    and we pray for all whom we love
    who are beyond our horizons and held in your care.

EASTER

Early on the first day of the week, while it was still dark, Mary of Magdala came to the tomb. She saw that the stone had been moved away from the entrance . . .

. . . Mary stood outside the tomb weeping. And as she wept, she peered into the tomb, and saw two angels in white sitting there, one at the head, and one at the feet, where the body of Jesus had lain.

They asked her, 'Why are you weeping?'
She answered, 'They have taken my Lord away, and I do not know where they have laid him'.

With these words she turned round and saw Jesus standing there, but she did not recognise him.
Jesus asked her, 'Why are you weeping? Who are you looking for?'

Thinking it was the gardener, she said, 'If it is you, sir, who removed him, tell me where you have laid him, and I will take him away'.

Jesus said, 'Mary!'

She turned and said to him, 'Rabbuni!' . . .

'Do not cling to me,' said Jesus, 'for I have not yet ascended to the Father. But go to my brothers, and tell them that I am ascending to my Father and your Father, to my God and your God.'

Mary of Magdala went to tell the disciples. 'I have seen the Lord!' she said, and gave them his message.

John 20:1, 11-18

Also Matthew 28:1-10; Mark 16:1-8; Luke 24:1-11.

Master!

It seems too good to be true!

But you come to us,
  call us by our name,
  joyfully laugh with us,
  – and it *is* true!

Living Lord,
  you were dead, really dead, dead and buried –

But God has raised you to life,
  and, with your risen life, begins a new creation!

By your resurrection
  the Father says 'Yes!' to all you said and did,
  does not annul Good Friday but confirms it!

Now we begin to see
  there is more to you than we realised,
  and more to life than we had known.

In this new burst of life,
  we find new perspectives, new light, new hope,
  a new world altogether.

On this best day of all, we celebrate;
  for you are loving us to life!

Living Lord,
  prove it is true:

  come to us now,
  call us by our name,
  breathe peace over us,
  and give us a new lease of life!

APPENDIX 1

EXPLANATORY NOTES

1. (page 12) JUDAS

It seems that Judas' betrayal of Jesus was provoked by the anointing at Bethany.

The tradition has been that Judas, who was treasurer (but not very trustworthy, according to John 12:6), betrayed Jesus because of his greed. But 30 shekels is worth less than £50 at current rates (1996). Other reasons seem more likely.

He may have become very disillusioned because Jesus rejected the violent revolt to which Judas' own fervent nationalism was committed.

Most likely, he was trying to provoke Jesus into such violent action – as in the meditations on pages 13 and 41.

JUDAS' EVIDENCE

The chief priests wanted two things: some way to arrest Jesus 'quietly' and some firm evidence against him. Judas could supply both.

He could lead them to the place at the right time; and he may have informed them about the 'anointing' at Bethany – which could be interpreted as 'being anointed king'. Only the high priest and the king were 'anointed': and, as Jesus was from the wrong tribe to be high priest, Mary's sensitive offering could have been distorted to represent a 'royal anointing'. It would be the firm evidence they needed to prosecute for treason.

2. (page 14) PASSOVER DATE

Any composite gospel such as this will present problems trying to reconcile contradictory accounts, dates and events.

For instance, there is clear disagreement between John and the other three gospels on the actual day of Passover (14th Nisan) that year.

Mark (14:12), Matthew and Luke set the Passover on the Thursday evening – with the lambs being slaughtered that afternoon; but John sets the Passover as beginning at sunset on the Friday – and the death of Jesus (whom John has always presented as the 'Lamb of God') coinciding with the killing of the lambs. In that case the meal in the Upper Room would be on the *eve* of Passover.

Who is right and how much they were each influenced by their own theological stance is open for discussion. What is clear is that their accounts are enriched rather than confused by their shaping of historical events in the light of their faith.

3. (page 16) WILDERNESS WAITING
John (10:22,40-42; 11:54; 12:1) may support the suggestion that Jesus was 'waiting in the wilderness' for almost three months before coming to Bethany just before Passover.

His 'Jerusalem ministry' began when he came to the harvest festival (Feast of Tabernacles) in October.

It would be typical of him if his 'triumphal entry' and the 'temple cleansing' were deliberately staged at the festival of the Dedication (in December) which celebrated the liberation when Judas Maccabaeus had a triumphal entry and purged the temple of Greek 'blasphemies'.

There would soon have been a warrant for Jesus' arrest and 'a price on his head'.

If all of that is sustained, then John's gospel supports the attractive idea that, when it was clear that he would be killed the next time he went to the city (John 11:16), Jesus withdrew to desert places *until the time he chose to hand himself over!*

A secret assassination in some dark place in January would not be acceptable: he wanted his death to be clearly linked with Passover (and his new Israel, new exodus, and his new Covenant). And so he was waiting in the wilderness until the time he *chose* to come to Jerusalem and let himself be taken.

Once again we see the distinctiveness of John. The Christ of the Fourth Gospel is not at the mercy of evil forces but controls his own destiny – and hands himself over in obedience to the Father.

4. (page 20) FEET-WASHING
Normally when invited to a meal in wealthier houses (like that of Mary of Jerusalem) there would be a servant waiting by the door to wash guests' feet as they entered. Open-toed sandals and dusty roads meant that, even though guests had washed before they set out, this feet-washing courtesy ensured refreshed comfort for them (and for their companions!) during the meal.

Jesus' insistence on secrecy and privacy for this meal presumably meant no servants were there – and none by the door. The Twelve were all aware of the omission but none had the humility to offer to serve the others.

When Simon objected to Jesus' action and tried to give it some sacramental significance, he was clearly reminded that Jesus was simply doing, and prepared to do, 'a servant's job'.

5. (page 22) PASSOVER SEATING
No table and chairs! They *reclined* (possibly on cushions) around a low 'table', and at angles to it, supported on their left elbows, eating with their right hands.

This meant the most trusted and privileged seat was on one's left – to whom one's back was exposed and onto whose breast one could lean back (as the beloved disciple on Jesus' right could lean back and speak confidentially to him – John 13:25).

Most significantly, Jesus had Judas on his left – in that special, trusted place.

6. (page 26) BREAD OF SACRIFICE
Passover centres on three pieces of unleavened bread and four cups of wine – as in the Seder on page 108.

The most important bread is the third – 'the bread of sacrifice' which is eaten with the main course of roast lamb.

There is a suggestion that the poorest families, who could not afford lamb, had to eat the Passover meal on the *eve* of Passover – and for them the bread *represented* the lamb.

Either way, it is this bread, traditionally linked with the lamb slain for deliverance, with which Jesus now identifies himself. He sees his approaching self-offering as that of the Lamb of God.

7. (page 29) ELIJAH
It is customary (as indicated in the Seder on page 108) to pour a fifth cup of wine – for Elijah – to refresh him on his expected return. And the youngest child goes to the door to see if he is coming, and leaves the door slightly ajar in welcome.

8. (page 40) ARREST
John's account of the arrest of Jesus differs from the other three – and clearly reflects the picture of Jesus which he wants to present.

He insists that Jesus is always in control of the situation. According to this gospel, Judas brings the soldiers to the garden but he does not kiss Jesus to identify him; Jesus hands himself over and asks that his disciples may go free.

The phrase 'when he was handed over' became very important in the theology and liturgy of the Church.

9. (page 52) CHARGE
Frustrated by the persistent silence of the accused and seeing no other way to get a response, the High Priest used the oath to which any faithful Jew must respond: 'I adjure you by the living God . . .', and got the response which he wanted.

10. (page 63) PEACE-MAKER
Dr Alan Dale in *New World*, his excellent N.T. translation for teenagers, wanted a 'description' of Jesus and paraphrased Paul's list of 'fruits of the Spirit' (Gal. 5:22) to describe this most Spirit-filled man. This includes the sentence, 'People who couldn't get on with one another found it possible to be friends in his presence' (*New World*, page 289).

11. (page 64) CROWD
Although it is often suggested that the people were especially fickle (shouting 'Hosanna' and then 'Crucify' within a few days), that may not be the case.

If, as suggested in note 3, there was a gap of some weeks between Palm Sunday and Jesus' arrest, there was time for people to become disillusioned and for Jesus to lose some support.

Few people are going to be on the streets at daybreak when the trial before Pilate begins! A 'rented crowd' seems more likely. It may well have been that, by the time word of these events had flashed round the markets, the sentence had been passed and was being carried out.

12. (page 70) SCOURGING
In John's account, Pilate takes the most unusual and irregular step of having Jesus scourged (with the subsequent mocking) before sentence has been passed.

This creates the only irreconcilable question in trying to compile a 'composite gospel'. In this devotional book I have stayed with the traditional order (as in Matthew and Mark) – so that 'scourging and mocking' follow the passing of the sentence.

It does, however, mean that I have had to omit the scene in which Pilate presents a 'scourged and mocked Jesus', looking at least pathetic and possibly ridiculous, to try to laugh the charges out of court (John 19:5). Pilate's announced 'Here is the man!' is most significant and ironic for St John: this man, despised by Jews and ridiculed by Pilate, is the 'true man', man as he is meant to be, 'the proper man' as Luther called him.

13. (page 72) MOCKING

With a plaited circlet of thorns so firmly established in Christian art and devotion, one is hesitant to mention a thorn-bush.

However, anyone who has made such a crown for a 'Passion play' (for instance) knows that it is a tricky task, needing some considerable time and some very stout gloves (which Roman soldiers did not have).

I am quite intrigued to see that in the much-discredited 'Turin shroud' the portrayed figure has upon his head (for some reason) a complete, upturned thorn-bush, roots and all.

So, although it may be most unwelcome, I must suggest that the soldiers did not have either the time nor the inclination to risk tearing their hands plaiting a crown, whatever Matthew and the others write.

It seems equally possible that when they had put the scarlet robe on him, and a reed in his hand, someone said, 'He ought to have a crown!', and one of them uprooted a thorn-bush and crushed it down, upturned, on his head – and they all laughed. They were not concerned with 'creating a devotion' but wanted to make him look as ridiculous as they could.

14. (page 74) CROSS

It is now generally thought that what prisoners were required to carry was the single heavy cross-beam which would make the horizontal. The vertical post or frame was already in place at execution hill.

However, the inscribed placard (which is now abbreviated to I.N.R.I.) would need to be nailed above his head, and that may vindicate the traditional Christian sign.

(page 79) What is quite clear, however, is that victims were not 'high and lifted up' as their feet were no more than two or three feet above the ground.

15. (page 76) SIMON

Mark would not have mentioned Alexander and Rufus unless

their names meant something to his readers – who traditionally were primarily the Christians in Rome.

And Paul, writing to Roman Christians, speaks of 'Rufus, chosen in the Lord, and his mother and mine'. This may well be the same Rufus. Both Paul and Mark could well be writing of Simon's family.

It can only be conjecture but it may well be that, being forced to share that burden, when he was probably on his way to the Temple, had a profound effect on Simon and his family.

16. (page 80) **I.N.R.I.**

I.N.R.I. is the traditional abbreviation for the Latin 'Iesus Nazarenus Rex Iudaeorum'; the inscription was also written in Latin and Greek.

It is also possible that Pilate was not gibing at the priests or 'wanting the last word' but expressing his contempt for all Jews if such a pathetic and degraded figure was their 'king'.

17. (page 82) **FORGIVING**

In *New World* (page 154) Dr Dale translates the Greek verb 'kept on praying'. Although there is only little support for this version from other translators, it is so consistent with the Man himself and with his teaching about prayer that I have retained it. And the grittiness of it made such impact on me when I first read it that this is how I now always 'hear' those words on Golgotha.

18. (page 88) **ELOI, ELOI**

Jesus' natural tongue was Aramaic, not Hebrew. This is one of only two occasions when the actual words which Jesus spoke are recorded and not translated into N.T. Greek.

It is also the only 'saying from the cross' which Mark records – and that underlines the extremity of Jesus' suffering.

APPENDIX 2

THE LAST SUPPER AND PASSOVER

The Passover Seder
Lighting the festival lights
1st CUP (Kiddush) poured and drunk

Hand-washing
Spring herbs in salt water
MATZA (unleavened bread) uncovered
1st MATZA shared
(children 'steal' and 'hide' half for later dessert)

2nd CUP (Haggadah) poured
Explanation of 'why this night above all others'
Lamb, matza, maror (herbs), charoset
Retelling of the story
Wine drunk

Ceremonial washing of hands
2nd MATZA with bitter herbs and charoset
Hillel sandwich dipped in charoset

3rd CUP (Thanksgiving) poured (drunk with meal)
3rd MATZA with main course of roast lamb, roast egg, vegetables
Dessert: includes Afikomen (Matza 'stolen' earlier)

Psalms
3rd cup drunk
Litany of blessings

4th CUP poured (and 5th for Elijah)
Hallel psalms
4th cup drunk
Psalms
Benedictions

Passover is *the* great celebration for Jews, a family festival of thanksgiving to God for his deliverance and founding and care of their nation.

Everything that is eaten in this meal and said at the table has deep symbolic significance and meaning, which you may easily identify in the Seder.

The most significant elements – roast lamb, unleavened bread, bitter herbs, and charoset (a paste representing mortar) – are specifically identified in the Seder in response to the questions of the youngest present.

Everything is introduced with a blessing. Jewish practice is not to bless *things* but to bless God for them: 'Blessed art thou, O Lord our God for . . .' is the regular thanksgiving throughout the meal.

The Seder (Order), which is printed on the opposite page, has remained unchanged for centuries. It centres on three pieces of Unleavened Bread which, together with four cups of wine (and a fifth for Elijah), make the framework of the meal.

The Supper in the Upper Room would have the same pattern and detail. But there are four points in the Seder which Jesus made very much his own by what he said and did.

1. FEET-WASHING

Early in the meal there are two occasions for hand-washing; the second is for the ceremonial washing of hands in obedience to the commandment.

This seems the most suitable point at which 'during supper' Jesus rose from the table, took off his outer garment, tied a towel round his waist, and began to wash his disciples' feet.

2. PREDICTION

Bitter herbs are dipped in charoset paste and eaten with a portion of the second piece of matza. There had also developed the custom of making a Hillel sandwich – bitter herbs between two bits of matza – and dipping that in the paste.

It was at this point that Jesus began to cry – and the disciples' questions led to his prediction that 'one who was dipping in the same bowl with him' would betray him.

3. THIS IS MY BODY

The third piece of matza accompanies the main course of roast lamb and roast egg, with vegetables.

Jesus took the bread eaten with (or perhaps representing) the lamb, slain for deliverance, and gives it his own new meaning:

'Blessed art Thou, O Lord, King of the universe, for bringing forth bread from the earth.'

(*and he broke the bread*)

'You see this bread of sacrifice. From now on, whenever you break bread like this, remember me; for my body will be broken, as this bread is broken, for the sake of the world. This is my body.'

4. THE NEW COVENANT

After the meal, some psalms, the third cup of wine and a litany of benedictions, the fourth cup of wine is poured (with Elijah's cup), and drunk after the singing of the Hallel psalms.

It is this cup that Jesus makes especially his own:

'You see this wine is red like blood. From now on, whenever you drink wine like this, remember me; for my blood is going to be shed for the forgiveness of sins. This cup is the New Covenant in my blood, shed for many.'

No wonder he was so determined that their meal should be in secret and not interrupted by those who were seeking him!

The new meanings which he brought to this traditional meal symbolised the new deliverance, the new Israel, and the New Covenant, which he believed would be accomplished by his self-offering.

He reduced that long and complex symbolic meal into the simplest symbolic meal, and made everyday things the signs of his sacrifice by which we celebrate his presence 'until he come'.

APPENDIX 3

USE IN HOLY WEEK

For several years, a selection of these readings and prayers has proved helpful in public worship on the evenings of Holy Week and on Good Friday.

We have used two voices, with a solo instrument (such as organ or clarinet) to make short interludes between different units, and short periods for silent prayer.

Sometimes the readings have been enhanced with the progressive extinguishing of Tenebrae candles, especially on Good Friday when all the readings from 'To Golgotha' to 'Good Friday' have been used.

On evenings earlier in the week, a selection of the earlier pages has been used to make a 'pilgrimage' from Bethany to Calvary, which is recommended for use in the worship of a local congregation.